Father's Day, The Poetry

Poetry is a fascinating use of language. With almost a million words at its command it is not surprising that these Isles have produced some of the most beautiful, moving and descriptive verse through the centuries. In this series we look at special days of celebration through the eyes and minds of our most gifted poets to bring you a guide to the days within each.

The role of Fathers has changed much over the course of centuries. Men are now better suited to a role of co-parent in this modern age rather than the stilted, slightly aloof figure of times past.

Being a Father is, of course, both a blessing and a burden. This modern day parenting in a frenetic fast changing world has to be both learnt and adapted from some inner well of memory from generations past as well as on the job experience. How to combine both the tenderness of love and support of modern views with the age old virtues of strength and leadership brings many difficulties to most men.

Surprisingly then that poets have given Fathers both a courageous view of life as well as a dependability to be there for their children. In success or failure we can identify with their hopes and dreams.

In this collection many of our greatest poets express their worded opinions of that unique role of Fatherhood – whether as one themselves or as a child reaching for that same mantle.

It's a difficult role for most men to assume and to keep perspective with but do you know any Father who is not ready to accept the challenge? Or any son and daughter not willing to acknowledge that unique and binding bond?

Many of the poems are also available as an audiobook from our sister company Portable Poetry. Many samples are at our youtube channel http://www.youtube.com/user/PortablePoetry?feature=mhee The full volume can be purchased from iTunes, Amazon and other digital stores. Among the readers are Tim Graham and Ghizela Rowe

INDEX OF TITLES

I Am Your Father - Daniel Sheehan
A Little Girl Lost - William Blake
Little Boy Lost - William Blake
Childless Father - William Wordsworth
Come Home Father - Henry Clay Work
On My First Son - Ben Jonson
Our Fathers Also - Rudyard Kipling
To My Father On His Birthday - Elizabeth Barrett Browning
Full Fathom Five - William Shakespeare
Epitaph Upon A Child That Died - Robert Herrick
To The Memory Of My Dear And Honoured Father - Anne Bradstreet
Our Fathers Of Old - Rudyard Kipling
Sonnet 37 - William Shakespeare
Portrait Of My Father As A Young Man - Rainer Maria Rilke
Of His Dear Son Gervase - Sir John Beaumont
My Serious Son - W S Landor
Oh Captain My Captain - Walt Whitman
To Her Father With Some Verses - Anne Bradstreet
My Fathers Chair - Rudyard Kipling
My Dearest Frank I Wish You Joy - Jane Austen
Alec Yeaten's Son - Thomas Bailey Aldrich
God Gave To Me A Child In Part - Robert Louis Stevenson
Come Up From The Fields Father - Walt Whitman
Seal Lullaby - Rudyard Kipling
Inscription - Eugene Field
Laus - Infantium - William Canton
My Hearts Leaps Up - William Wordsworth
To An Infant - Samuel Taylor Coleridge
Sweet And Low - Alfred Lord Tennyson

Etude Realiste - Algernon Charles Swinburne

A Baby's feet, like sea-shells pink,
Might tempt, should heaven see meet,
An angel's lips to kiss, we think,
A baby's feet.

Like rose-hued sea-flowers toward the heat
They stretch and spread and wink
Their ten soft buds that part and meet.

No flower-bells that expand and shrink
Gleam half so heavenly sweet
As shine on life's untrodden brink
A baby's feet.

A baby's hands, like rosebuds furled
Whence yet no leaf expands,
Ope if you touch, though close upcurled,
A baby's hands.

Then, fast as warriors grip their brands
When battle's bolt is hurled,
They close, clenched hard like tightening bands.

No rosebuds yet by dawn impearled
Match, even in loveliest lands,
The sweetest flowers in all the world -
A baby's hands.

A baby's eyes, ere speech begin,
Ere lips learn words or sighs,
Bless all things bright enough to win
A baby's eyes.

Love, while the sweet thing laughs and lies,
And sleep flows out and in,
Sees perfect in them Paradise.

Their glance might cast out pain and sin,
Their speech make dumb the wise,
By mute glad godhead felt within
A baby's eyes.

Any Father To Any Son - F. B. T. Money-Coutts

For thee a crown of thorns I wear.
And thought imperative constrains
My labouring heart for thee to bear
The travail of a woman's pains ;

For with intolerable presage
Of all the amazements of thy life.
The pits of ancient woe I gauge,
The vast impediments of strife ;

Or else in dreadful dreaming cast,
I see thy form before me fly,
By prescience never overpast
Nor fleetest foot that love can ply.

Still as thy shadow must I run,
When all the shadows fall behind,
And in the rich seductive sun
Thou to the darker bars art blind,

Any Soldier To His Son - Anonymous

What did I do, sonny, in the Great World War?
Well, I learned to peel potatoes and to scrub the barrack floor.
I learned to push a barrow and I learned to swing a pick,
I learned to turn my toes out, and to make my eyeballs click.
I learned the road to Folkestone, and I watched the English shore,
Go down behind the skyline, as I thought, for evermore.
And the Blighty boats went by us and the harbour hove in sight,
And they landed us and sorted us and marched us "by the right".
"Quick march!" across the cobbles, by the kids who rang along
Singing "Appoo?" "Spearmant" "Shokolah?" through dingy old Boulogne;
By the widows and the nurses and the niggers and Chinese,
And the gangs of smiling Fritzes, as saucy as you please.

I learned to ride as soldiers ride from Etaps to the Line,
For days and nights in cattle trucks, packed in like droves of swine.
I learned to curl and kip it on a foot of muddy floor,
And to envy cows and horses that have beds of beaucoup straw.
I learned to wash in shell holes and to shave myself in tea,
While the fragments of a mirror did a balance on my knee.
I learned to dodge the whizz-bangs and the flying lumps of lead,
And to keep a foot of earth between the sniper and my head.
I learned to keep my haversack well filled with buckshee food,
To take the Army issue and to pinch what else I could.

I learned to cook Maconochie with candle-ends and string,
With "four-by-two" and sardine-oil and any God-dam thing.
I learned to use my bayonet according as you please
For a breadknife or a chopper or a prong for toasting cheese.
I learned "a first field dressing" to serve my mate and me
As a dish-rag and a face-rag and a strainer for our tea.
I learned to gather souvenirs that home I hoped to send,
And hump them round for months and months and dump them in the end.
I learned to hunt for vermin in the lining of my shirt,
To crack them with my finger-nail and feel the beggars spirt;
I learned to catch and crack them by the dozen and the score
And to hunt my shirt tomorrow and to find as many more.

I learned to sleep by snatches on the firestep of a trench,
And to eat my breakfast mixed with mud and Fritz's heavy stench.
I learned to pray for Blighty ones and lie and squirm with fear,
When Jerry started strafing and the Blighty ones were near.
I learned to write home cheerful with my heart a lump of lead
With the thought of you and mother, when she heard that I was dead.
And the only thing like pleasure over there I ever knew,
Was to hear my pal come shouting, "There's a parcel, mate, for you."

So much for what I did do - now for what I have not done:
Well, I never kissed a French girl and I never killed a Hun,
I never missed an issue of tobacco, pay, or rum,
I never made a friend and yet I never lacked a chum.

I never borrowed money, and I never lent - but once
(I can learn some sorts of lessons though I may be borne a dunce).
I never used to grumble after breakfast in the Line
That the eggs were cooked too lightly or the bacon cut too fine.
I never told a sergeant just exactly what I thought,
I never did a pack-drill, for I never quite got caught.
I never punched a Red-Cap's nose (be prudent like your Dad),
But I'd like as many sovereigns as the times I've wished I had.
I never stopped a whizz-bang, though I've stopped a lot of mud,
But the one that Fritz sent over with my name on was a dud.
I never played the hero or walked about on top,
I kept inside my funk hole when the shells began to drop.
Well, Tommy Jones's father must be made of different stuff:
I never asked for trouble - the issue was enough.

So I learned to live and lump it in the lovely land of war,
Where the face of nature seems a monstrous septic sore,
Where the bowels of earth of earth hang open, like the guts of something slain,
And the rot and wreck of everything are churned and churned again;
Where all is done in darkness and where all is still in day,
Where living men are buried and the dead unburied lay;
Where men inhabit holes like rats, and only rats live there;
Where cottage stood and castle once in days before La Guerre;
Where endless files of soldiers thread the everlasting way,
By endless miles of duckboards, through endless walls of clay;
Where life is one hard labour, and a soldiers gets his rest
When they leave him in the daisies with a puncture in his chest;
Where still the lark in summer pours her warble from the skies,
And underneath, unheeding, lie the blank upstaring eyes.

And I read the Blighty papers, where the warriors of the pen
Tell of "Christmas in the trenches" and "The Spirit of our men";
And I saved the choicest morsels and I read them to my chum,
And he muttered, as he cracked a louse and wiped it off his thumb:
"May a thousand chats from Belgium crawl under their fingers as they write;
May they dream they're not exempted till they faint with mortal fright;
May the fattest rats in Dickebusch race over them in bed;
May the lies they've written choke them like a gas cloud till they're dead;
May the horror and the torture and the things they never tell
(For they only write to order) be reserved for them in Hell!"

You'd like to be a soldier and go to France some day?
By all the dead in Delville Wood, by all the nights I lay
Between our lines and Fritz's before they brought me in;
By this old wood-and-leather stump, that once was flesh and skin;
By all the lads who crossed with me but never crossed again,
By all the prayers their mothers and their sweethearts prayed in vain,
Before the things that were that day should ever more befall
May God in common pity destroy us one and all!

Faith And Despondency - Emily Jane Brontë

The winter wind is loud and wild,
Come close to me, my darling child;
Forsake thy books, and mateless play;
And, while the night is gathering grey,
We'll talk its pensive hours away;

'Ierne, round our sheltered hall
November's gusts unheeded call;
Not one faint breath can enter here
Enough to wave my daughter's hair,
And I am glad to watch the blaze
Glance from her eyes, with mimic rays;
To feel her cheek so softly pressed,
In happy quiet on my breast.

'But, yet, even this tranquillity
Brings bitter, restless thoughts to me;
And, in the red fire's cheerful glow,
I think of deep glens, blocked with snow;
I dream of moor, and misty hill,
Where evening closes dark and chill;
For, lone, among the mountains cold,
Lie those that I have loved of old.
And my heart aches, in hopeless pain
Exhausted with repinings vain,
That I shall greet them ne'er again!'

'Father, in early infancy,
When you were far beyond the sea,
Such thoughts were tyrants over me!
I often sat, for hours together,
Through the long nights of angry weather,
Raised on my pillow, to descry
The dim moon struggling in the sky;

Or, with strained ear, to catch the shock,
Of rock with wave, and wave with rock;
So would I fearful vigil keep,
And, all for listening, never sleep.
But this world's life has much to dread,
Not so, my Father, with the dead.

'Oh! not for them, should we despair,
The grave is drear, but they are not there;
Their dust is mingled with the sod,
Their happy souls are gone to God!
You told me this, and yet you sigh,
And murmur that your friends must die.
Ah! my dear father, tell me why?

For, if your former words were true,

How useless would such sorrow be;
As wise, to mourn the seed which grew
Unnoticed on its parent tree,
Because it fell in fertile earth,
And sprang up to a glorious birth
Struck deep its root, and lifted high
Its green boughs, in the breezy sky.

'But, I'll not fear, I will not weep
For those whose bodies rest in sleep,
I know there is a blessed shore,
Opening its ports for me, and mine;
And, gazing Time's wide waters o'er,
I weary for that land divine,
Where we were born, where you and I
Shall meet our Dearest, when we die;
From suffering and corruption free,
Restored into the Deity.'

'Well hast thou spoken, sweet, trustful child!
And wiser than thy sire;
And worldly tempests, raging wild,
Shall strengthen thy desire
Thy fervent hope, through storm and foam,
Through wind and ocean's roar,
To reach, at last, the eternal home,
The steadfast, changeless, shore!'

The Parable Of The Old Man And The Young - Wilfred Owen

So Abram rose, and clave the wood, and went,
And took the fire with him, and a knife.
And as they sojourned both of them together,
Isaac the first-born spake and said, My Father,
Behold the preparations, fire and iron,
But where the lamb for this burnt-offering?
Then Abram bound the youth with belts and strops,
And builded parapets and trenches there,
And stretched forth the knife to slay his son.
When lo! an angel called him out of heaven,
Saying, Lay not thy hand upon the lad,
Neither do anything to him. Behold,
A ram, caught in a thicket by its horns;
Offer the Ram of Pride instead of him.

But the old man would not so, but slew his son,
And half the seed of Europe, one by one.

That Endless Loop - Daniel Sheehan

That Endless Loop,
That endless loop keeps playing now
Just round and round and round again.
I haven't counted now the times
Your last breath, sleeping eyes awake,
Caught the dryness of your throat
And rasped itself past famished lips so sore

That loop keeps playing now
And seconds, minutes, hours become the days
Since you are gone.
So long have you been gone now Father dear
That I now see in this eternity of void
The future when my children let ME go
To somewhere not yet known, that exist may not
Except inside ourselves as memories
As pictures.... videos of days gone by.

I watched the clock stay its hands at 9 and 20,
Then I heard my Mother call your name,
My brother gulp before the cry,
My sister blink the tears to know the end,
And my words 'He's gone now Mum"
And you had.
And nieces, nephews knew the flame
Had gone from deep within.
Extinguished, empty now your body stilled
And you escaped, became the ether
Or went to Heaven....anywhere but here.
With us.
With me.

Oh Daddy dear now you're gone and my eyes watch
The World in different ways
I hear a different song and time expands
Oh daddy dear I know that what I'm feeling now will pass
But I remember watching how you slept in pain
In ward and room and know the end was near
And listened to your words cracked with
Pain but full of care.

I would wander to your side when others went
To be with you to fill the moments
Such as now when you are gone.
And now you are.
I remember trying to close your eyes and wishing
Silently inside that you blink awake
and hold my hand

I still recall my words so raised and loud
In the ward declaring; 'now you walk' and 'now you eat'
Willing you to beat this thing that riddled you within.

But one day knowing that we would tend you at your side
With time the enemy of our moments left
But also now the saviour who would vanquish pain
From deep inside of you

Now you are gone, daddy dear
And I know that soon this loop will stop
And the memories of our time before
Will seep back in and suffuse our lives again

My children know your name and will forever know
That Grandad did not live in vain
They will remember you and treasure you through me
And what you left inside of me.
Go now Daddy dear and know that you have left,
Your flesh and blood, your son, with your greatest gift -
The gift of life and with it all your love.
Go now Daddy dear for life must carry on
Go now Daddy dear but listen gently for my words
That from my heart will carry through to you
Wherever you may be –
In heaven
In the wind
The trees and sun
You are with me in my actions and my thoughts
I will carry on what you have begun.
Go now Daddy dear – I will always be my Father's son.

Epitaph On My Ever Honoured Father - Robert Burns

O Ye whose cheek the tear of pity stains,
Draw near with pious rev'rence, and attend!
Here lie the loving husband's dear remains,
The tender father, and the gen'rous friend;
The pitying heart that felt for human woe,
The dauntless heart that fear'd no human pride;
The friend of man-to vice alone a foe;
For "ev'n his failings lean'd to virtue's side."

Lord Ullin's Daughter - Thomas Campbell

A chieftain, to the highlands bound,
Cries, `Boatman, do not tarry!
And I'll give thee a silver pound
To row us o'er the ferry!''

`Now, who be ye, would cross Lochgyle,
This dark and stormy weather?''
`O, I'm the chief of Ulva's isle,

And this, Lord Ullin's daughter.

`And fast before her father's men
Three days we've fled together,
For should he find us in the glen,
My blood would stain the heather.

`His horsemen hard behind us ride;
Should they our steps discover,
Then who will cheer my bonny bride
When they have slain her lover?"

Out spoke the hardy Highland wight,
`I'll go, my chief--I'm ready:
It is not for your silver bright;
But for your winsome lady:

`And by my word! the bonny bird
In danger shall not tarry;
So, though the waves are raging white,
I'll row you o'er the ferry."

By this the storm grew loud apace,
The water-wraith was shrieking;
And in the scowl of heaven each face
Grew dark as they were speaking.

But still as wilder blew the wind,
And as the night grew drearer,
Adown the glen rode armèd men,
Their trampling sounded nearer.

`O haste thee, haste!" the lady cries,
`Though tempests round us gather;
I'll meet the raging of the skies,
But not an angry father."

The boat has left a stormy land,
A stormy sea before her,
When, O! too strong for human hand,
The tempest gather'd o'er her.

And still they row'd amidst the roar
Of waters fast prevailing:
Lord Ullin reach'd that fatal shore,
His wrath was changed to wailing.

For, sore dismay'd through storm and shade,
His child he did discover:
One lovely hand she stretch'd for aid,
And one was round her lover.

`Come back! come back!'' he cried in grief
`Across this stormy water:
And I'll forgive your Highland chief,
My daughter! O my daughter!''

'Twas vain: the loud waves lash'd the shore,
Return or aid preventing:
The waters wild went o'er his child,
And he was left lamenting.

A Poet's Welcome To His Love Begotten Daughter – Robert Burns

Thou's welcome, wean; mishanter fa' me,
If thoughts o' thee, or yet thy mamie,
Shall ever daunton me or awe me,
My bonie lady,
Or if I blush when thou shalt ca' me
Tyta or daddie.

Tho' now they ca' me fornicator,
An' tease my name in kintry clatter,
The mair they talk, I'm kent the better,
E'en let them clash;
An auld wife's tongue's a feckless matter
To gie ane fash.

Welcome! my bonie, sweet, wee dochter,
Tho' ye come here a wee unsought for,
And tho' your comin' I hae fought for,
Baith kirk and queir;
Yet, by my faith, ye're no unwrought for,
That I shall swear!

Wee image o' my bonie Betty,
As fatherly I kiss and daut thee,
As dear, and near my heart I set thee
Wi' as gude will
As a' the priests had seen me get thee
That's out o' hell.

Sweet fruit o' mony a merry dint,
My funny toil is now a' tint,
Sin' thou came to the warl' asklent,
Which fools may scoff at;
In my last plack thy part's be in't
The better ha'f o't.

Tho' I should be the waur bestead,
Thou's be as braw and bienly clad,
And thy young years as nicely bred
Wi' education,

As ony brat o' wedlock's bed,
In a' thy station.

Lord grant that thou may aye inherit
Thy mither's person, grace, an' merit,
An' thy poor, worthless daddy's spirit,
Without his failins,
'Twill please me mair to see thee heir it,
Than stockit mailens.

For if thou be what I wad hae thee,
And tak the counsel I shall gie thee,
I'll never rue my trouble wi' thee,
The cost nor shame o't,
But be a loving father to thee,
And brag the name o't

I Am Your Father – By Daniel Sheehan

I am your father
And you are my children
When all that I have done, can do, for you
Is enough, it is not enough for me.
In hours and days and weeks between
I give my time to make the time for you
To grow, to love, to share the
Thoughts and dreams of all your ages
I am your father and in times now past my Will be done
But now is now and you are you and I am I
And what matters is that our hearts be done.

I want mine to know the joy of all your love
To know that I am your Father and that I am your Friend
I want yours to know that above all else
The sacrifice I make for you I make with a smile
For it is no sacrifice at all to know that you are well and loved
And that I am your Father
And you are my children

A Little Girl Lost - William Blake

Children of the future age,
Reading this indignant page,
Know that in a former time
Love, sweet love, was thought a crime.

In the age of gold,
Free from winter's cold,
Youth and maiden bright,
To the holy light,

Naked in the sunny beams delight.

Once a youthful pair,
Filled with softest care,
Met in garden bright
Where the holy light
Had just removed the curtains of the night.

Then, in rising day,
On the grass they play;
Parents were afar,
Strangers came not near,
And the maiden soon forgot her fear.

Tired with kisses sweet,
They agree to meet
When the silent sleep
Waves o'er heaven's deep,
And the weary tired wanderers weep.

To her father white
Came the maiden bright;
But his loving look,
Like the holy book
All her tender limbs with terror shook.

'Ona, pale and weak,
To thy father speak!
Oh the trembling fear!
Oh the dismal care
That shakes the blossoms of my hoary hair!'

The Little Boy Lost - William Blake

"Father, father, where are you going?
Oh do not walk so fast!
Speak, father, speak to you little boy,
Or else I shall be lost."

The night was dark, no father was there,
The child was wet with dew;
The mire was deep, and the child did weep,
And away the vapour flew.

The Childless Father - William Wordsworth

"Up, Timothy, up with your staff and away!
Not a soul in the village this morning will stay;
The hare has just started from Hamilton's grounds,
And Skiddaw is glad with the cry of the hounds."

Of coats and of jackets grey, scarlet, and green,
On the slopes of the pastures all colours were seen;
With their comely blue aprons, and caps white as snow,
The girls on the hills made a holiday show.

Fresh sprigs of green box-wood, not six months before,
Filled the funeral basin at Timothy's door;
A coffin through Timothy's threshold had past;
One Child did it bear, and that Child was his last.

Now fast up the dell came the noise and the fray,
The horse and the horn, and the hark! hark away!
Old Timothy took up his staff, and he shut
With a leisurely motion the door of his hut.

Perhaps to himself at that moment he said;
"The key I must take, for my Ellen is dead."
But of this in my ears not a word did he speak;
And he went to the chase with a tear on his cheek.

Come Home, Father! - Henry Clay Work

'Tis The Song of Little Mary,
Standing at the bar-room door
While the shameful midnight revel
Rages wildly as before.

Father, dear father, come home with me now!
The clock in the steeple strikes one;
You said you were coming right home from the shop,
As soon as your day's work was done.
Our fire has gone out our house is all dark
And mother's been watching since tea,
With poor brother Benny so sick in her arms,
And no one to help her but me.
Come home! come home! come home!
Please, father, dear father, come home.

Hear the sweet voice of the child
Which the night winds repeat as they roam!
Oh who could resist this most plaintive of prayers?
"Please, father, dear father, come home."

Father, dear father, come home with me now!
The clock in the steeple strikes two;
The night has grown colder, and Benny is worse
But he has been calling for you.
Indeed he is worse Ma says he will die,
Perhaps before morning shall dawn;
And this is the message she sent me to bring

"Come quickly, or he will be gone."
Come home! come home! come home!
Please, father, dear father, come home.

Hear the sweet voice of the child
Which the night winds repeat as they roam!
Oh who could resist this most plaintive of prayers?
"Please, father, dear father, come home."

Father, dear father, come home with me now!
The clock in the steeple strikes three;
The house is so lonely the hours are so long
For poor weeping mother and me.
Yes, we are alone poor Benny is dead,
And gone with the angels of light;
And these were the very last words that he said
"I want to kiss Papa good night."
Come home! come home! come home!
Please, father, dear father, come home.

Hear the sweet voice of the child
Which the night winds repeat as they roam!
Oh who could resist this most plaintive of prayers?
"Please, father, dear father, come home."

On My First Son - Benjamin Jonson

Farewell, thou child of my right hand, and joy;
My sin was too much hope of thee, loved boy.
Seven years thou wert lent to me, and I thee pay,
Exacted by thy fate, on the just day.

Oh, could I lose all father now! For why
Will man lament the state he should envy?
To have so soon 'scaped world's and flesh's rage,
And if no other misery, yet age!

Rest in soft peace, and asked, say, Here doth lie
Ben Jonson his best piece of poetry.
For whose sake henceforth all his vows be such
As what he loves may never like too much.
Thrones, Powers, Dominions, Peoples, Kings,
Are changing 'neath our hand.
Our fathers also see these things
But they do not understand.

By--they are by with mirth and tears,
Wit or the works of Desire-

Cushioned about on the kindly years
Between the wall and the fire.

Our Fathers Also - Rudyard Kipling

Thrones, Powers, Dominions, Peoples, Kings,
Are changing 'neath our hand.
Our fathers also see these things
But they do not understand.

By--they are by with mirth and tears,
Wit or the works of Desire-
Cushioned about on the kindly years
Between the wall and the fire.

The grapes are pressed, the corn is shocked
Standeth no more to glean;
For the Gates of Love and Learning locked
When they went out between.

All lore our Lady Venus bares,
Signalled it was or told
By the dear lips long given to theirs
And longer to the mould.

All Profit, all Device, all Truth,
Written it was or said
By the mighty men of their mighty youth,
Which is mighty being dead.

The film that floats before their eyes
The Temple's Veil they call;
And the dust that on the Shewbread lies
Is holy over all.

Warn them of seas that slip our yoke,
Of slow-conspiring stars-
The ancient Front of Things unbroke
But heavy with new wars?

By--they are by with mirth and tears,
Wit or the waste of Desire-
Cushioned about on the kindly years
Between the wall and the fire!

To My Father On His Birthday - Elizabeth Barrett Browning

Amidst the days of pleasant mirth,
That throw their halo round our earth;
Amidst the tender thoughts that rise

To call bright tears to happy eyes;
Amidst the silken words that move
To syllable the names we love;
There glides no day of gentle bliss
More soothing to the heart than *this!*
No thoughts of fondness e'er appear
More fond, than those I write of here!
No name can e'er on tablet shine,
My father more beloved than *thine!*
'Tis sweet, adown the shady past,
A lingering look of love to cast--
Back th' enchanted world to call,
That beamed around us first of all;
And walk with Memory fondly o'er
The paths where Hope had been before--
Sweet to receive the sylphic sound
That breathes in tenderness around,
Repeating to the listening ear

The names that made our childhood dear--
For parted Joy, like Echo, kind,
Will leave her dulcet voice behind,
To tell,amidst the magic air,
How oft she smiled and lingered there.

Full Fathom Five - William Shakespeare

Full fathom five thy father lies;
Of his bones are coral made;
Those are pearls that were his eyes:
Nothing of him that doth fade
But doth suffer a sea-change
Into something rich and strange.
Sea-nymphs hourly ring his knell:
Ding-dong.
Hark! now I hear them,--ding-dong, bell.

Epitaph Upon A Child That Died – Robert Herrick

Here she lies, a pretty bud,
Lately made of flesh and blood:
Who as soon fell fast asleep
As her little eyes did peep.
Give her strewings, but not stir
The earth that lightly covers her.

**To The Memory Of My Dear And Ever Honored Father Thomas Dudley Esq
- Anne Bradstreet.**

By duty bound, and not by custom led
To celebrate the praises of the dead,
My mournful mind, sore pressed, in trembling verse
Presents my lamentations at his hearse
Who was my father, guide, instructor, too,
To whom I ought whatever I could do.

Nor is it relation near my hand shall tie;
For who more cause to boast his worth than I?
Who heard, or saw, observed, or knew him better,
Or who alive than I a greater debtor ?
Let malice bite, and envy gnaw its fill,
He was my father, and I praise him still.

Nor was his name or life led so obscure
That pity might some trumpeters procure,
Who after death might make him falsely seem
Such as in life no man could justly deem.

Well known and loved, where ere he lived, by most,
Both in his native and in foreign coast,
These to the world his merits could make known,
So need no testimonial from his own.

But now or never I must pay my sum;
While others tell his worth, I will not be dumb.
One of thy founders him, New England, know,
Who stayed thy feeble sides when thou wast low,
Who spent his state, his strength, and years with care
That aftercomers in them might have share.

True patriot of this little commonweal,
Who is it can tax thee aught but for thy zeal ?
Truth s friend thou wert, to errors still a foe,
Which caused apostates to malign thee so.
Thy love to true religion e er shall shine
My father s God be God of me and mine!

Upon the earth he did not build his nest,
But as a pilgrim what he had possessed.
High thoughts he gave no harbor in his heart,
Nor honors puffed him up, when he had part;
Those titles loathed which some too much do love,
For truly his ambition lay above.

His humble mind so loved humility
He left it to his race for legacy,
And oft and oft, with speeches mild and wise,
Gave his in charge that jewel rich to prize.
No ostentation seen in all his ways,
As in the mean ones of our foolish days,
Which all they have, and more, still set to view

Their greatness may be judged by what they show.
His thoughts were more sublime, his actions wise;
Such vanities he justly did despise.

"Our Fathers of Old" - Rudyard Kipling

Excellent herbs had our fathers of old
Excellent herbs to ease their pain
Alexanders and Marigold,
Eyebright, Orris, and Elecampane
Basil, Rocket, Valerian, Rue,
(Almost singing themselves they run)
Vervain, Dittany, Call-me-to-you
Cowslip, Melilot, Rose of the Sun.
Anything green that grew out of the mould
Was an excellent herb to our fathers of old.

Wonderful tales had our fathers of old,
Wonderful tales of the herbs and the stars
The Sun was Lord of the Marigold,
Basil and Rocket belonged to Mars.
Pat as a sum in division it goes
(Every herb had a planet bespoke)
Who but Venus should govern the Rose?
Who but Jupiter own the Oak?
Simply and gravely the facts are told
In the wonderful books of our fathers of old.

Wonderful little, when all is said,
Wonderful little our fathers knew.
Half their remedies cured you dead
Most of their teaching was quite untrue
"Look at the stars when a patient is ill.
(Dirt has nothing to do with disease),
Bleed and blister as much as you will,
Bister and bleed him as oft as you please."
Whence enormous and manifold
Errors were made by our fathers of old.

Yet when the sickness was sore in the land,
And neither planets nor herbs assuaged,
They took their lives in their lancet-hand
And, oh, what a wonderful war they waged!
Yes, when the crosses were chalked on the door-
(Yes, when the terrible dead-cart rolled!)
Excellent courage our fathers bore
None too learned, but nobly bold
Into the fight went our fathers of old.

If it be certain, as Galen says

And sage Hippocrates holds as much
"That those afflicted by doubts and dismays
Are mightily helped by a dead man's touch,"
Then, be good to us, stars above!
Then, be good to us, herbs below!
We are afflicted by what we can prove,
We are distracted by what we know.
So-ah, so!
Down from your heaven or up from your mould
Send us the hearts of our Fathers of old!

Sonnet 37: As A Decrepit Father Takes Delight - William Shakespeare

As a decrepit father takes delight
To see his active child do deeds of youth,
So I, made lame by Fortune's dearest spite,
Take all my comfort of thy worth and truth.
For whether beauty, birth, or wealth, or wit,
Or any of these all, or all, or more,
Entitled in thy parts, do crownèd sit,
I make my love engrafted to this store.
So then I am not lame, poor, nor despised,
Whilst that this shadow doth such substance give
That I in thy abundance am sufficed
And by a part of all thy glory live.
Look what is best, that best I wish in thee.
This wish I have; then ten times happy me!

Portrait Of My Father As A Young Man - Rainer Maria Rilke

In the eyes: dream. The brow as if it could feel
something far off. Around the lips, a great
freshness--seductive, though there is no smile.
Under the rows of ornamental braid
on the slim Imperial officer's uniform:
the saber's basket-hilt. Both hands stay
folded upon it, going nowhere, calm
and now almost invisible, as if they
were the first to grasp the distance and dissolve.
And all the rest so curtained within itself,
so cloudy, that I cannot understand
this figure as it fades into the background.

Oh quickly disappearing photograph
in my more slowly disappearing hand.

Of His Dear Son, Gervase - Sir John Beaumont
Dear Lord, receive my son, whose winning love
To me was like a friendship, far above

The course of nature or his tender age;
Whose looks could all my bitter griefs assuage:
Let his pure soul, ordain'd seven years to be
In that frail body which was part of me,
Remain my pledge in Heaven, as sent to show
How to this port at every step I go.

My Serious Son - W S Landor.

My serious son ! I see thee look
First on the picture, then the book.
I catch the wish that thou couldst paint
The yearnings of the ecstatic saint.
Give it not up, my serious son
Wish it again, and it is done.
Seldom will any fail who tries
With patient hand and steadfast eyes,
And woos the true with such pure sighs.

O Captain! My Captain! - Walt Whitman

O Captain! my Captain! our fearful trip is done;
The ship has weather'd every rack, the prize we sought is won;
The port is near, the bells I hear, the people all exulting,
While follow eyes the steady keel, the vessel grim and daring:
But O heart! heart! heart!
O the bleeding drops of red,
Where on the deck my Captain lies,
Fallen cold and dead.

O Captain! my Captain! rise up and hear the bells;
Rise up--for you the flag is flung--for you the bugle trills;
For you bouquets and ribbon'd wreaths--for you the shores a-crowding;
For you they call, the swaying mass, their eager faces turning;
Here Captain! dear father!
This arm beneath your head;
It is some dream that on the deck,
You've fallen cold and dead.

My Captain does not answer, his lips are pale and still;
My father does not feel my arm, he has no pulse nor will;
The ship is anchor'd safe and sound, its voyage closed and done;
From fearful trip, the victor ship, comes in with object won; 20
Exult, O shores, and ring, O bells!
But I, with mournful tread,
Walk the deck my Captain lies,
Fallen cold and dead.

To Her Father, With Some Verses - Anne Bradstreet

Most truly honored, and as truly dear,
If worth in me or aught I do appear
Who can of right better demand the same
Than may your worthy self, from whom it came?
The principal might yield a greater sum,
Yet, handled ill, amounts but to this crumb.
My stock s so small I know not how to pay,
My bond remains in force unto this day;
Yet for part payment take this simple mite.
Where nothing s to be had kings lose their right.
Such is my debt I may not say " Forgive! "
But as I can I Ml pay it while I live;
Such is my bond none can discharge but I,
Yet, paying, is not paid until I die.

My Father's Chair - Rudyard Kipling
Parliaments of Henry III., 1265

There are four good legs to my Father's Chair
Priests and People and Lords and Crown.
I sits on all of 'em fair and square,
And that is reason it don't break down.

I won't trust one leg, nor two, nor three,
To carry my weight when I sets me down.
I wants all four of 'em under me
Priests and People and Lords and Crown.

I sits on all four and favours none
Priests, nor People, nor Lords, nor Crown:
And I never tilts in my chair, my son,
And that is the reason it don't break down.

When your time comes to sit in my Chair,
Remember your Father's habits and rules,
Sit on all four legs, fair and square,
And never be tempted by one-legged stools!

My Dearest Frank, I Wish You Joy - Jane Austen

My dearest Frank, I wish you joy
Of Mary's safety with a Boy,
Whose birth has given little pain
Compared with that of Mary Jane.
May he a growing Blessing prove,
And well deserve his Parents' Love!
Endow'd with Art's and Nature's Good,
Thy Name possessing with thy Blood,

In him, in all his ways, may we
Another Francis WIlliam see!
Thy infant days may he inherit,
THey warmth, nay insolence of spirit;
We would not with one foult dispense
To weaken the resemblance.
May he revive thy Nursery sin,
Peeping as daringly within,
His curley Locks but just descried,
With 'Bet, my be not come to bide.'
Fearless of danger, braving pain,
And threaten'd very oft in vain,
Still may one Terror daunt his Soul,
One needful engine of Controul
Be found in this sublime array,
A neigbouring Donkey's aweful Bray.
So may his equal faults as Child,
Produce Maturity as mild!
His saucy words and fiery ways
In early Childhood's pettish days,
In Manhood, shew his Father's mind
Like him, considerate and Kind;
All Gentleness to those around,
And anger only not to wound.
Then like his Father too, he must,
To his own former struggles just,
Feel his Deserts with honest Glow,
And all his self-improvement know.
A native fault may thus give birth
To the best blessing, conscious Worth.
As for ourselves we're very well;
As unaffected prose will tell.
Cassandra's pen will paint our state,
The many comforts that await
Our Chawton home, how much we find
Already in it, to our mind;
And how convinced, that when complete
It will all other Houses beat
The ever have been made or mended,
With rooms concise, or rooms distended.
You'll find us very snug next year,
Perhaps with Charles and Fanny near,
For now it often does delight us
To fancy them just over-right us.

Alec Yeaton's Son - Thomas Bailey Aldrich

The wind it wailed, the wind it moaned,
And the white caps flecked the sea;
"An' I would to God," the skipper groaned,
"I had not my boy with me!

Snug in the stern-sheets, little John
Laughed as the scud swept by;
But the skipper's sunburnt cheeks grew wan
As he watched the wicked sky.

"Would he were at his mother's side!"
And the skipper's eyes were dim.
"Good Lord in heaven, if ill betide,
What would become of him!

"For me--my muscles are as steel,
For me let hap what may;
I might make shift upon the keel
Until the break o' day.

"But he, he is so weak and small,
So young, scarce learned to stand-
O pitying Father of us all,
I trust him in Thy hand!

"For Thou, who makest from on high
A sparrow's fall each one!
Surely, O Lord, thou'lt have an eye
On Alec Yeaton's son!"

Then, helm hard-port; right straight he sailed
Towards the headland light:
The wind it moaned, the wind it wailed,
And black, black fell the night.

Then burst a storm to make one quail
Though housed from winds and waves
They who could tell about that gale
Must rise from watery graves!

Sudden it came, as sudden went;
Ere half the night was sped,
The winds were hushed, the waves were spent,
And the stars shone overhead.

Now, as the morning mist grew thin,
The folk on Gloucester shore
Saw a little figure floating in
Secure, on a broken oar!

Up rose the cry, "A wreck! a wreck!
Pull, mates, and waste no breath!"
They knew it, though 't was but a speck
Upon the edge of death!

Long did they marvel in the town

At God his strange decree,
That let the stalwart skipper drown
And the little child go free!

God Gave To Me A Child In Part - Robert Louis Stevenson

God gave to me a child in part,
Yet wholly gave the father's heart:
Child of my soul, O whither now,
Unborn, unmothered, goest thou?

You came, you went, and no man wist;
Hapless, my child, no breast you kist;
On no dear knees, a privileged babbler, clomb,
Nor knew the kindly feel of home.

My voice may reach you, O my dear-
A father's voice perhaps the child may hear;
And, pitying, you may turn your view
On that poor father whom you never knew.

Alas! alone he sits, who then,
Immortal among mortal men,
Sat hand in hand with love, and all day through
With your dear mother wondered over you.

Come Up From the Fields Father - Walt Whitman

Come up from the fields father, here's a letter from our Pete,
And come to the front door mother, here's a letter from thy
dear son.

Lo, 'tis autumn,
Lo, where the trees, deeper green, yellower and redder,

Cool and sweeten Ohio's villages with leaves fluttering in the
moderate wind,
Where apples ripe in the orchards hang and grapes on the
trellis'd vines,
(Smell you the smell of the grapes on the vines?
Smell you the buckwheat where the bees were lately buzzing?)

Above all, lo, the sky so calm, so transparent after the rain,
and with wondrous clouds,
Below too, all calm, all vital and beautiful, and the farm
prospers well.

Down in the fields all prospers well,
But now from the fields come father, come at the daughter's call,
And come to the entry mother, to the front door come right away.

Fast as she can she hurries, something ominous, her steps trembling,
She does not tarry to smooth her hair nor adjust her cap.

Open the envelope quickly,
O this is not our son's writing, yet his name is sign'd,
O a strange hand writes for our dear son, O stricken mother's soul!
All swims before her eyes, flashes with black, she catches the
main words only,
Sentences broken, gunshot wound in the breast, cavalry
skirmish, taken to hospital,
At present low, but will soon be better.

Ah now the single figure to me,
Amid all teeming and wealthy Ohio with all its cities and farms,
Sickly white in the face and dull in the head, very faint,
By the jamb of a door leans.

Grieve not so, dear mother, (the just-grown daughter speaks
through her sobs,
The little sisters huddle around speechless and dismay'd,)
See, dearest mother, the letter says Pete will soon be better.
Alas poor boy, he will never be better, (nor may-be needs to
be better, that brave and simple soul,)
While they stand at home at the door he is dead already,
The only son is dead.

But the mother needs to be better,
She with thin form presently drest in black,
By day her meals untouch'd, then at night fitfully sleeping,
often waking,
In the midnight waking, weeping, longing with one deep longing,
O that she might withdraw unnoticed, silent from life escape and withdraw,
To follow, to seek, to be with her dear dead son.

Seal Lullaby - Rudyard Kipling

Oh! hush thee, my baby, the night is behind us
And black are the waters that sparkled so green.
The moon, O'er the combers, looks downward to find us
At rest in the hollows that rustle between.
Where billow meets billow, there soft by the pillow.
Oh, weary wee flipperling, curl at thy ease!
The storm shall not wake thee, no shark shall overtake thee
Asleep in the storm of slow-swinging seas.

Inscription For My Little Son's Silver Plate - Eugene Field

When thou dost eat from off this plate,
I charge thee be thou temperate;

Unto thine elders at the board
Do thou sweet reverence accord;
And, though to dignity inclined,
Unto the serving-folk be kind;
Be ever mindful of the poor,
Nor turn them hungry from the door;
And unto God, for health and food
And all that in thy life is good,
Give thou thy heart in gratitude.

Laus Infantium - William Canton

In praise of little children I will say
God first made man, then found a better way
For woman, but his third way was the best.
Of all created things, the loveliest
And most divine are children. Nothing here
Can be to us more gracious or more dear.
And though, when God saw all his works were good,
There was no rosy flower of babyhood,
'T was said of children in a later day
That none could enter Heaven save such as they.
The earth, which feels the flowering of a thorn,
Was glad, O little child, when you were born;
The earth, which thrills when skylarks scale the blue,
Soared up itself to God's own Heaven in you;

And Heaven, which loves to lean down and to glass
Its beauty in each dewdrop on the grass,—
Heaven laughed to find your face so pure and fair,
And left, O little child, its reflex there.

My Heart Leaps Up - William Wordsworth

My heart leaps up when I behold
A rainbow in the sky:
So was it when my life began;
So is it now I am a man;
So be it when I shall grow old,
Or let me die!
The Child is father of the Man;
And I could wish my days to be
Bound each to each by natural piety.

To An Infant - Samuel Taylor Coleridge

Ah ! cease thy tears and sobs, my little Life
I did but snatch away the unclasped knife :
Some safer toy will soon arrest thine eye,

And to quick laughter change this peevish cry!
Poor stumbler on the rocky coast of Woe,
Tutored by Pain each source of pain to know I
Alike the foodful fruit and scorching fire
Awake thy eager grasp and young desire ;
Alike the Good, the III offend thy sight.
And rouse the stormy sense of shrill Affright !
Untaught, yet Avise ! 'mid all thy brief alarms
Thou closely elingest to thy Mother's arms.
Nestling thy little face in that fond breast
Whose anxious heavings lull thee to thy rest
Man's breathing Miniature ! thou mak'st me sigh —
A Babe art thou — and such a Thing am I!

To anger rapid and as soon appeased,
For trifles mourning and by trifles pleased,
Break Friendship's mirror with a tetchy blow,
Yet snatch what coals of fire on Pleasure's altar glow !
O thou that rearest with celestial aim
The future Seraph in my mortal frame,
Thrice holy Faith ! whatever thorns I meet
As on I totter with unpractised feet,
Still let me stretch my arms and cling to thee,
Meek nurse of souls through their long Infancy !

Sweet And Low - Alfred Lord Tennyson

Sweet and low, sweet and low,
Wind of the western sea,
Low, low, breathe and blow,
Wind of the western sea!
Over the rolling waters go,
Come from the dying moon, and blow,
Blow him again to me;
While my little one, while my pretty one, sleeps.

Sleep and rest, sleep and rest,
Father will come to thee soon;
Rest, rest, on mother's breast,
Father will come to thee soon;
Father will come to his babe in the nest,
Silver sails all out of the west
Under the silver moon:
Sleep, my little one, sleep, my pretty one, sleep.

www.ingramcontent.com/pod-product-compliance
Lightning Source LLC
Chambersburg PA
CBHW070951040426
42443CB00012B/3300